Best Free Open Source

Data Recovery Apps for Mac OS

English Edition

by

Cyber Jannah Sakura

2023

Cyber Jannah Sakura Publishing

2023

Prologue

Mac OS, developed by Apple Computer have rich history spanning over three decades. It originated in 1984 as Macintosh System Software, providing a graphical user interface for Apple's Macintosh computers. Over time, it evolved through various iterations, including Mac OS 9 and Mac OS X, before transitioning to a Unix-based foundation with Mac OS X 10.0.

Subsequent versions brought significant enhancements, such as Spotlight, Time Machine, and the Mac App Store. In 2012, Apple introduced Mac OS, renaming the operating system. It continues to receive regular updates, introducing new features, improved performance, and enhanced security, catering to the evolving needs of Mac users.

Data recovery app for macOS is a software application designed to retrieve lost or deleted files from Mac computers and storage devices. These apps utilize advanced algorithms and techniques to scan the storage media for traces of lost data and attempt to recover them. They can handle various data loss scenarios, including accidental deletion, formatting, corruption, and system crashes.

Data recovery apps for macOS typically support a wide range of file systems and storage devices, such as internal and external hard drives, solid-state drives (SSDs), USB drives, SD cards, and more. They often provide features like quick and deep scanning, file preview, selective recovery, and the ability to restore different file types, including documents, photos, videos, music, and archives. The goal of these apps is to help users retrieve their lost or inaccessible data, whether it's due to human error, hardware failure, or other unforeseen circumstances, and restore it back to their Mac computers or other storage devices.

1. TestDisk Recovery App

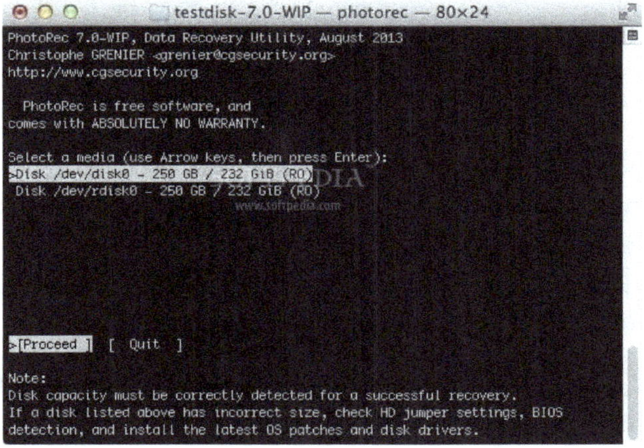

TestDisk is a free and open-source data recovery utility that is compatible with macOS and several other operating systems. While TestDisk is primarily a command-line tool, it also has a companion application called PhotoRec, which provides a graphical user interface for easier data recovery on macOS.

Data Recovery: TestDisk focuses on data recovery from various storage devices, including hard drives, SSDs, USB drives, memory cards, and more. It can help recover lost or deleted partitions, files, and folders from damaged or formatted storage media.

Partition Recovery: TestDisk is particularly useful for recovering lost or deleted partitions on a disk. It can detect and rebuild damaged or overwritten partition tables, allowing users to access their lost data.

File System Support: TestDisk supports a wide range of file systems, including popular ones like NTFS, FAT32, exFAT, HFS+, APFS, and ext family (ext2, ext3, ext4). This broad compatibility enables data recovery from different file system formats.

Free and Open-Source: TestDisk are free and open-source software, which means they can be used without any cost and their source code is publicly available. This allows for transparency, community contributions, and ongoing development.

TestDisk are trusted tools for data recovery, known for their reliability and effectiveness. However, they require some technical knowledge and understanding to operate effectively. It is advisable to read the documentation and follow the instructions carefully when using these tools for data recovery on macOS.

Link Download

https://www.cgsecurity.org/wiki/TestDisk

2. PhotoRec Recovery App

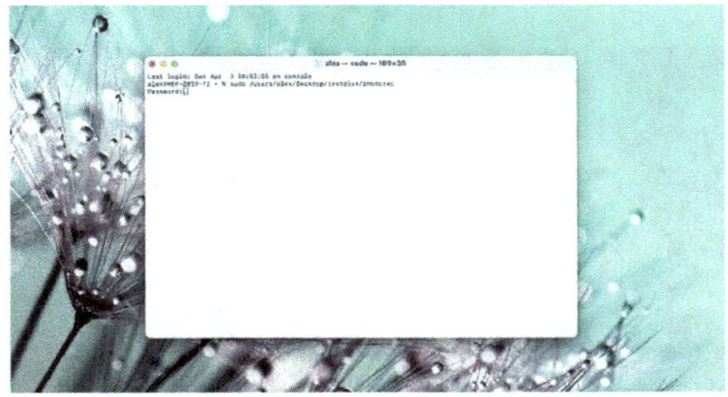

PhotoRec is a free and open-source data recovery software that is compatible with macOS, among other operating systems.

It is a companion application to TestDisk and is specifically designed for recovering various types of multimedia files, including photos, videos, and audio files, from formatted or damaged storage media.

Link Download

https://www.cgsecurity.org/wiki/PhotoRec

3. Foremost Recovery App

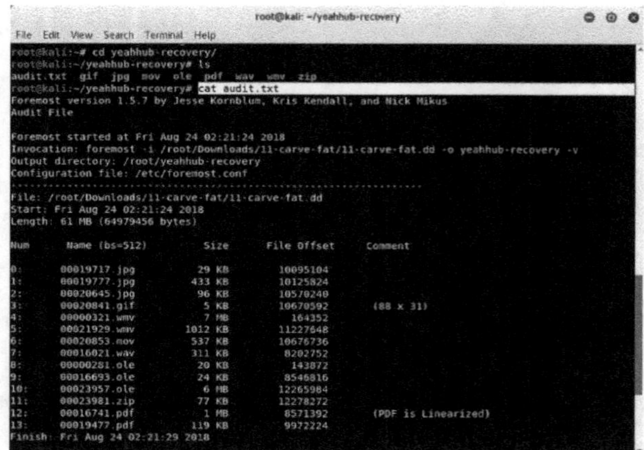

Foremost is a command-line data recovery utility that can be used on macOS and other operating systems. It is designed to recover files based on their headers, footers, and internal data structures.

While Foremost does not have a graphical user interface, it offers a flexible and customizable approach to file recovery.

Here are some key features of Foremost:

File Recovery: Foremost is primarily focused on file recovery, aiming to retrieve deleted or lost files from storage devices such as hard drives, SSDs, USB drives, and memory cards. It can recover a wide range of file types, including documents, images, videos, audio files, and more.

Header/Footer-Based Recovery: Foremost uses file signatures and headers/footers to identify and recover specific file types. It analyzes the content of the storage media and attempts to reconstruct files based on their known structures.

Customizable Configuration: Foremost provides extensive configuration options, allowing users to specify the file types they want to recover. It uses customizable configuration files to define file headers, footers, and other parameters for accurate recovery.

Command-Line Interface: Foremost operates entirely through a command-line interface, requiring users to provide specific commands and parameters to initiate and customize the recovery process. This may require some familiarity with the command-line environment.

Cross-Platform Compatibility: Foremost is cross-platform software and can be used on macOS, Linux, and other operating systems. This makes it a versatile option for data recovery across different platforms.

Free and Open-Source: Foremost is distributed as free and open-source software, allowing users to use it without any cost. Its source code is publicly available, encouraging transparency, community contributions, and ongoing development.

Foremost is a powerful and flexible data recovery tool, particularly suited for advanced users who are comfortable with the command-line interface and have specific file recovery requirements.

While it may require some technical expertise to utilize effectively, Foremost can be a valuable tool for recovering specific file types on macOS and other operating systems.

Link Download

https://github.com/korczis/foremost

4. Scalpel Recovery App

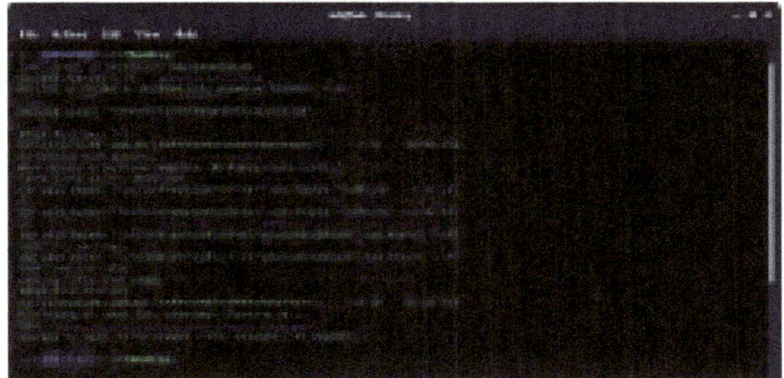

Scalpel is a command-line data recovery utility that can be used on macOS and other operating systems. It is designed to recover files based on file carving techniques, analyzing the data on storage devices to identify and extract specific file types. Scalpel is known for its accuracy and customizable configuration options.

Link Download

https://github.com/sleuthkit/scalpel

5. Disk Drill Recovery App

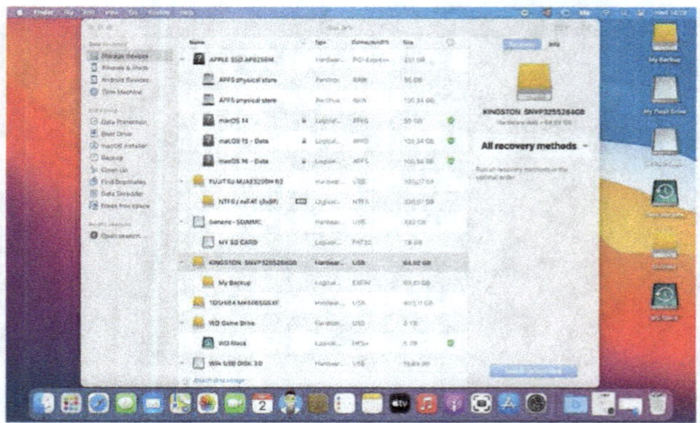

Disk Drill is a popular data recovery application for macOS that offers both free and paid versions. It provides a user-friendly interface and a range of features for recovering lost or deleted files from various storage devices.

Quick and Deep Scans: Disk Drill offers both quick and deep scanning options to cater to different data loss scenarios. The quick scan can swiftly locate recently deleted files, while the deep scan thoroughly searches the storage device for more complex data recovery situations.

Multiple File System Support: Disk Drill supports a wide range of file systems, including HFS, HFS+, APFS, FAT, and NTFS. This broad compatibility enables data recovery from different file system formats, making it versatile for various storage devices.

Recovery Vault and Guaranteed Recovery: Disk Drill includes a Recovery Vault feature that works in the background, creating a secure database of metadata to improve the chances of successful file recovery. The Guaranteed Recovery feature allows users to create a copy of selected files to ensure their recoverability.

Preview and Filter: Disk Drill provides a file preview option that allows users to preview recoverable files before performing the actual recovery. It also offers filtering options to search for specific file types or file attributes, simplifying the recovery process.

Partition Recovery and Rebuild: Disk Drill can recover lost or deleted partitions on storage devices. It also has the ability to rebuild damaged or corrupted partitions, helping users regain access to their data.

S.M.A.R.T. Monitoring: Disk Drill includes S.M.A.R.T. (Self-Monitoring, Analysis, and Reporting Technology) monitoring to detect and warn users about potential disk failures or issues. This helps users take preventive measures and protect their data.

Additional Tools: Disk Drill offers additional tools, such as disk cleanup, duplicate finder, and data backup options. These tools help users manage and optimize their storage devices.

Link Download

https://www.cleverfiles.com/

6. R-Studio for Mac Recovery App

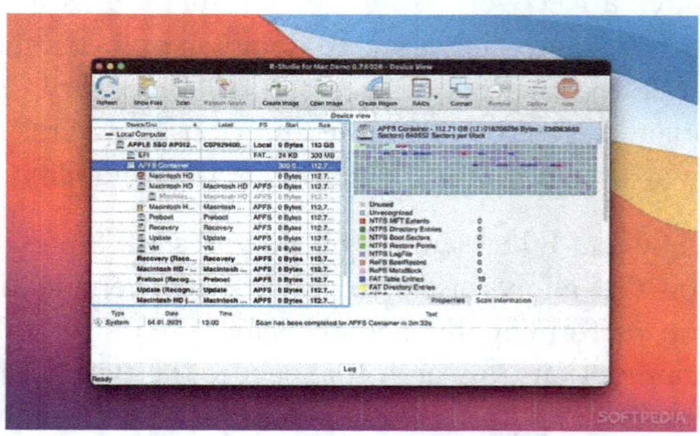

R-Studio for Mac is a comprehensive data recovery software designed specifically for macOS. It is a powerful application that allows users to recover lost or deleted files from various storage devices, including internal and external hard drives, SSDs, USB drives, and RAID arrays.

Advanced Data Recovery: R-Studio for Mac utilizes advanced algorithms and techniques to scan storage devices for recoverable files. It can recover data lost due to accidental deletion, formatting, partition loss, file system corruption, virus attacks, and other data loss scenarios.

Multiple File System Support: The software supports a wide range of file systems, including HFS/HFS+/APFS (Mac), FAT/FAT32/exFAT (Windows), NTFS (Windows), and more. This allows for effective recovery from different file system formats.

RAID Data Recovery: R-Studio for Mac is capable of recovering data from various RAID configurations, including RAID 0, RAID 1, RAID 5, RAID 6, and RAID 10. It can handle both software and hardware RAID recoveries.

Flexible Scan Options: R-Studio for Mac offers flexible scanning options, including quick scan and deep scan. The quick scan option is faster and suitable for recent data loss, while the deep scan option thoroughly searches the storage device for more complex data recovery situations.

Remote Data Recovery: The software supports remote data recovery, allowing users to recover data from a remote computer over a network connection. This can be particularly useful in situations where physical access to the storage device is not possible.

Cross-Platform Compatibility: R-Studio for Mac is compatible with both macOS and Windows, allowing users to recover data from Mac-formatted storage devices on Windows computers and vice versa.

Link Download

https://www.rstudio.com/data_recovery_macintosh/Download.shtml

7. DMDE Recovery App

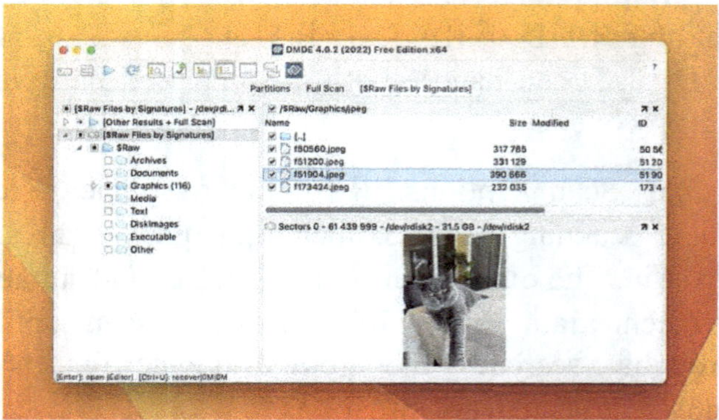

DMDE (DM Disk Editor and Data Recovery Software) is a powerful data recovery application that is compatible with macOS, Windows, and Linux. It provides advanced features for disk editing, partition management, and data recovery from various storage devices.

Disk and Partition Editing: DMDE allows users to perform low-level disk editing, enabling them to view and modify disk structures, including partitions, file systems, and boot sectors. It provides tools for creating, deleting, resizing, and formatting partitions.

File Recovery: DMDE specializes in data recovery and can retrieve deleted or lost files from different storage devices, such as hard drives, SSDs, USB drives, memory cards, and RAID arrays. It supports various file systems, including NTFS, FAT, exFAT, HFS+, APFS, and ext family (ext2, ext3, ext4).

Partition Recovery: DMDE can recover lost or deleted partitions, including those that have been accidentally formatted or damaged due to partition table corruption. It can rebuild partition tables and restore access to lost data.

File Carving and Signature Search: DMDE utilizes file carving techniques to recover files by analyzing the raw data on storage devices. It can search for file signatures and footers to identify and extract specific file types, even if the file system information is lost or corrupted.

Disk Imaging and Cloning: DMDE allows users to create disk images or make exact clones of disks or partitions. This feature is useful for creating backups or working with data preservation purposes.

Hexadecimal and Text Viewers: DMDE includes built-in viewers for hexadecimal and text data, enabling users to analyze and interpret raw disk data or examine file contents at a low level.

Support for Encrypted and Virtual Disks: DMDE supports the recovery of files from encrypted disks and virtual disk images, providing access to data stored in TrueCrypt, BitLocker, FileVault, and other encrypted formats.Link Download

Link Download

https://dmde.com/download.html

8. Lazesoft Mac Data Recovery App

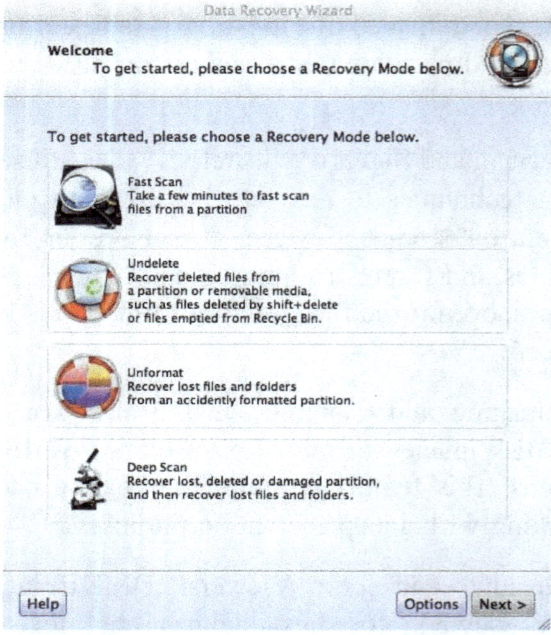

Lazesoft Mac Data Recovery is a user-friendly data recovery application specifically designed for macOS. It offers a range of features and tools to help users recover lost or deleted files from various storage devices.

File Recovery: Lazesoft Mac Data Recovery allows users to recover accidentally deleted or lost files from hard drives, SSDs, USB drives, memory cards, and other storage devices. It supports a wide range of file types, including documents, photos, videos, music files, and more.

Multiple Recovery Modes: The software offers different recovery modes to cater to different data loss situations. It includes a fast scan mode for quick file recovery and a deep scan mode for more thorough scanning and recovery of fragmented or overwritten files.

Partition Recovery: Lazesoft Mac Data Recovery can also recover lost or deleted partitions on storage devices. It can detect and restore damaged or corrupted partition tables, helping users regain access to their data.

Preview and Selective Recovery: The application provides a preview function that allows users to preview recoverable files before performing the actual recovery. This feature helps ensure the accuracy and integrity of the recovered files. Users can also selectively recover specific files or folders, rather than recovering the entire data set.

Bootable Recovery Media: Lazesoft Mac Data Recovery allows users to create a bootable recovery CD or USB drive. This feature is useful in situations where the macOS installation is not accessible or when recovering data from a non-bootable system.

Simple and Intuitive Interface: The software features a user-friendly interface with step-by-step instructions, making it accessible to users with varying levels of technical expertise. It simplifies the data recovery process and guides users through the necessary steps.

Free Version: Lazesoft Mac Data Recovery offers a free version with limited features, allowing users to evaluate the software and recover a limited amount of data at no cost. A premium version with advanced features and unlimited data recovery is also available for purchase

Link Download

www.macdatarecoveryfreeware.com

9. EaseUS Data Recovery Wizard for Mac App

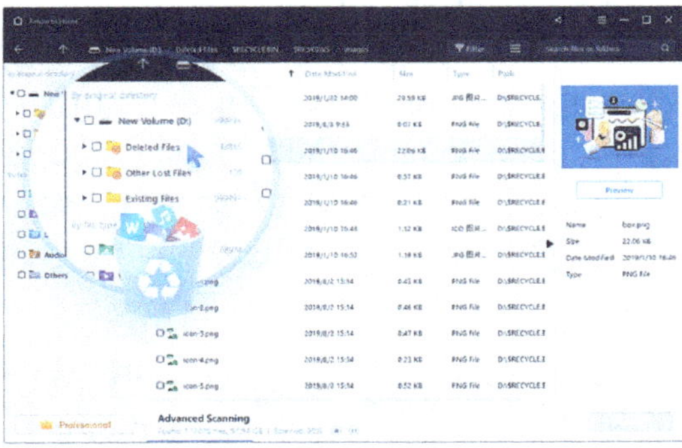

EaseUS Data Recovery Wizard for Mac is a comprehensive data recovery application specifically designed for macOS. Basic version its free and it offers a user-friendly interface and a wide range of features to help users recover lost or deleted files from various storage devices.

File Recovery: The software allows users to recover accidentally deleted, formatted, or lost files from Mac computers, external hard drives, SSDs, USB drives, memory cards, and other storage devices. It supports a wide variety of file types, including documents, photos, videos, audio files, emails, and more.

Quick and Deep Scan: EaseUS Data Recovery Wizard for Mac offers both quick and deep scanning options. The quick scan can quickly locate recently deleted files, while the deep scan thoroughly searches the storage device for more complex data recovery scenarios, including formatted or inaccessible drives.

Preview and Selective Recovery: The application provides a preview feature that allows users to preview recoverable files before proceeding with the recovery process. This helps ensure the accuracy and integrity of the recovered files. Users can also selectively recover specific files or folders, saving time and storage space.

Bootable Media: EaseUS Data Recovery Wizard for Mac enables users to create a bootable media (USB or DVD) for data recovery in case the macOS installation is not accessible or when recovering data from a non-bootable system.

Multiple File System Support: The software supports various file systems, including HFS, HFS+, APFS, FAT, exFAT, and NTFS. It can recover data from different file system formats, making it compatible with a wide range of storage devices.

Recover from Time Machine Backups: EaseUS Data Recovery Wizard for Mac can also recover files directly from Time Machine backups. This feature is useful when users have a Time Machine backup available and only need to recover specific files or folders.

Link Download

https://www.easeus.com/mac-data-recovery-software/drw-mac-free.htm

10. Mac Data Recovery Guru App

Mac Data Recovery Guru is a data recovery application specifically developed for macOS. It offers a simple and intuitive interface along with a range of features to assist users in recovering lost or deleted files from Mac computers and various storage devices.

Real-Time File Preview: Mac Data Recovery Guru offers a unique feature that allows users to preview recoverable files in real-time during the scanning process. This feature helps users identify and select the files they want to recover, saving time and improving efficiency.

Selective Recovery: Users can choose to selectively recover specific files or folders rather than recovering the entire data set. This feature enables users to focus on recovering the most important files, minimizing the recovery time and storage space required.

File Filtering and Sorting: The application includes advanced file filtering and sorting options, enabling users to refine the search results based on file attributes such as name, size, date modified, and more. This makes it easier to locate and recover specific files.

Easy-to-Use Interface: Mac Data Recovery Guru features a user-friendly interface that does not require any technical expertise. The straightforward design and intuitive navigation make it accessible to users with varying levels of computer knowledge.

Efficient and Lightweight: The software is designed to be efficient and lightweight, ensuring minimal impact on system resources during the data recovery process. This allows users to continue using their Mac computers for other tasks while the recovery is in progress.

Link Download

https://macosxfilerecovery.com/

Conclusion

It's important to note that data recovery can be a complex and delicate process, and the success of recovery depends on various factors.

It is recommended to carefully read the documentation and instructions provided with each tool and consider seeking professional assistance for critical data recovery scenarios.

References

O'Malley, Kevin (2003). Programming Mac OS X: A Guide for Unix Developers. Manning. ISBN 1-930110-85-5.

Williams, Justin (March 11, 2008). Getting StartED with Mac OS X Leopard. Apress. ISBN 978-1-4302-0519-7.

Tanenbaum, A. & Woodhull, A. S. (1997). Operating Systems: Design And Implementation, 2nd ed. New York: Prentice Hall.

"Data Recovery – Backup Technology". www.dell.com. Archived from the original on 1 December 2022.

Author Bio

Open Source Indie App Developer & Self Publisher
Author from Blue Planet Terra